Up Late Reading *Birds of America*

Up Late Reading *Birds of America*

Robert DeMott

Sheila-Na-Gig Editions
2021

Copyright © 2021 Robert DeMott

Author photo: © Kate Fox

Cover art: John James Audubon, *American Crow* (1833), plate #CLVI of *The Birds of America*

ISBN: 978-1-7354002-7-3

Sheila-Na-Gig Editions
www.sheilanagigblog.com

ALL RIGHTS RESERVED
Printed in the United States of America

By Robert DeMott

Works

Angling Days: A Fly Fisher's Journals (2016; 2019)
Steinbeck's Typewriter: Essays on His Art (1996; 2012)
Brief and Glorious Transit: Prose Poems (2007)
Steinbeck's Reading (1984; 2007)
Dave Smith: A Literary Archive (2000)
The Weather in Athens: Poems (2001)
News of Loss: Poems (1995)

Edited Anthologies

Conversations with Jim Harrison (2002; Revised and Updated 2019)
Astream: American Writers on Fly Fishing (2012)
Afield: American Writers on Bird Dogs (2010) [with Dave Smith]
After The Grapes of Wrath: *Essays on John Steinbeck* (1995)
    [with Donald Coers and Paul Ruffin]
Artful Thunder: Versions of the Romantic Tradition in American Literature (1975) [with Sanford Marovitz]
From Athens Out (1974) [with Carol Harter]

Editions of John Steinbeck's Writings

Sweet Thursday (2008)
Travels with Charley *and Later Novels, 1947-1962* (2007)
    [with Brian Railsback]
The Grapes of Wrath (2006)
Novels, 1942-1952 (2001)
The Grapes of Wrath *and Other Writings, 1936-1941* (1996)
Novels and Stories, 1932-1937 (1994)
Working Days: The Journals of The Grapes of Wrath, *1938-1941* (1989)

For Elizabeth, Kate, Brandi, Isabella, and Olivia:
hearts of my heart

"Tell all the sands and every blade of grass

Please tell the wind to let my love pass...."

—Rex Garvin, "Over the Mountain; Across the Sea"

(sung by Johnnie and Joe)

"Se Dio lo vuole."

—Philomena Ventrella

Acknowledgments

A number of these poems appeared earlier in different form in *The Weather in Athens,* in *Brief and Glorious Transit,* in a Territorial Press Broadside, hand printed by Aaron Parrett, in *Essentially Athens,* and in these journals: *Place, Yale Angler's Journal, Heartlands, Riverwind, ISLE: Interdisciplinary Studies in Literature and Environment, Lake Effect, Gray's Sporting Journal, Reed, Sheila-Na-Gig online,* and *Limberlost Review.* Special thanks to Kate Fox for her keen eye and unflagging intelligence.

Contents

Once	11
Profligate Rain: An Incident	12
Whine Of Marriage	14
Influx Of Waxwings	16
North	18
A River In Wyoming	20
At The Armor Museum	22
The Year Dylan Went Electric	24
The Invention Of Cruelty	26
Rimbaud, Falling	29
Quadtych, With Place Names	31
Up Late Reading *Birds Of America*	35
During A War	37
The Dredge At Alder Gulch	40
Near Last Chance	42
At The Turn Of This Century	44
Nebraska Letter	47
The World Is But Whirligig	49
Moscow: Novodevichy Convent	51
Christmas This Year	53
In Our 75th Winter	55
Falling Asleep Over Lowell	58
It Is What It Is	60
Yellow Trillium Brown Trout Rusty Spinner	62
Everything Gets Lost In Translation	64
In The Corner Room	66

"The thing that eats the heart comes wild with years."
—Stanley Kunitz

"Where's the gizmoness?"
—Indian Larry (aka Lawrence DeSmedt),
old school chopper maven

Once

Years ago, at dusk on Christmas Eve,
in those few minutes of day left before loved ones
arrived for evening's ritual of giving and getting,
I walked outside, under a woolen batt of sky,
and hauled buckets of bird seed with enough
to fill each feeder in our woodsy backyard—
black oil sunflower for one, thistle for another,
millet and pumpkin seed for a third. You
get the drift: I was spreading good cheer
as I dipped and ladled at each station
along my route, carefully stopping here and there
to sweep away empty seed husks and corn cobs
left by marauding crows, jays, and squirrels,
for once asking nothing for myself, when,
out of deepening shadows and *tick-tick* of falling sleet,
a pair of black-capped chickadees, dressed to the nines
in stylish evening garb, lit on my bare hand,
pecked seed from its open palm, so close
in that sweet moment, I swear I heard
the thrum of their pistoned hearts,
but it has nearly always been enough....

Profligate Rain: An Incident

> "...all was vanity and a striving after wind...."
> —*Ecclesiastes* 2:11

One night, in warp and woof of greenest, lushest summer, your labors beneath the sun done for the day, and everybody else in the household absent or otherwise occupied, you are making a test of pleasure, sitting alone in a quiet nook, a cozy anteroom, reading a book of the inner spirit and trying to write in measured strokes of what you thought to find there, though nothing comes, until, that is, an old-time storm rolls into town, a juggernaut, the kind your elders always warned you about but you refused to believe could happen, not to you, not in suburbia, anyway: roof-shaking thunder and torrent of biblical proportions, then sea tide in gutters, oceanic backwash down plaster ceilings and walls, followed by hail, another fist in your face: *Where does it come from, where does it go, this profligate rain, this angry deluge, squandering itself like a slaphappy lover all over town?* It's then a brood of chimney swifts (you never knew such homely things existed) knocked from their mortared moorings inside the old brick fireplace, come sailing their sooty coffins into your living room, out over the white hooked Berber rug, family heirloom, wedding gift you couldn't help prizing above all else, though everyone told you you should have known better. You run for a dustpan and broom, sweep up each blackened body, though a few, mouths agape, are still flapping blindly in a purling river of ash. Beyond the detritus and now-silent judgment of animals, the moment goes on, borne on the wind, ink streaks on a scribbled page of diary. And only then you think you know what your next move will be....

WHINE OF MARRIAGE

Suffering from heat, cranky, intemperate, some old philosopher said: what is it but the one life to be fucked up as you go? Sure, and this is yours, your story as of this place and moment, for which, fill in the blanks. Let's say mid-August in a typical Midwestern river town: no end of wind-blown rain, thunder showers, and hideous green spore-bloom: mildew and mold colonizing every unlit corner of the house, even shoes and belts peppered with swamp snow. You think you'd know the drill by now: doze off, then wake every few minutes, vertiginous, the line between dream and not-dream blurred in your head, your limbs contorted, night clothes awash in sweat. A leather-bound copy of *The Art of Love* leers from the nightstand. Next to it a nearly empty tumbler of bourbon. You wonder how anyone can be sleeping in such unholy weather. All week your secrets unraveled and tonight on a sour shuck mattress they scream aloud. Gothic, this torture, absolutely Gothic, though you know somewhere out there someone has it worse and you shouldn't complain. Perspective is all, you want to believe. Downstairs, the old Waterbury clock, a wedding present from someone whose name you can't recall, unwinds in decadent moisture: its limp clapping gong tolls from further and further depths until at last, it might as well be be chiming underwater, its percussion become a muted obbligato, leaden counterpoint to a furious voice hovering near your bed, steady stream of accusations, barrage of protests. How fantasia of night goes on forever in those lost choices—love and duty, yours and mine, thrust and parry, tit for tat—stuttering in the idiot blink of the clock radio, like a heart dismantling, thump by weary thump, in liquid darkness. Whatever words you have die in the wheeze of ceiling fans. Face it: this is your story right now, chapter and verse unreviseable: there are no apologies for anger, no solace for doubts or speaking in tongues this seventh night of prodigal deluge, so you turn your back, close your eyes, and pray for a high dry wind to scour rafter and roof beam, so you can tell yourself what you don't quite believe, that in time, *this too will pass.*

Influx Of Waxwings

> " A delirium of birds!"
> —Theodore Roethke

On a dark morning, coldest day this season, when hearts are most sere and brittle, when all is turned inward toward zero and vacant embraces of nothing, suddenly there is movement in the front yard trees, flashes of color and noise outside our ice-glazed bedroom. Then, startled from isolate sleep, pouty and sullen, trailing thick clouds, we remember the day and rise slowly to watch, as though this were the only pleasure we are likely to have. Once each year, like clockwork, in deep January, borne down on high winds from Lake Erie, a gang of masked troubadours wheels into our little hick town. First nothing, then something: flocks of thirty or forty, gaily bedecked, elegantly dressed vagabonds on the lam from their boreal houses and cathedrals of pine. In an instant cedar waxwings are everywhere we would imagine them to be banqueting like royalty on fermented clusters of wild grape, last remaining pips of orange bittersweet, and blood-red fruit of our female holly trees. *Have not, want not,* we tell each other, drawing close: soon so much bounty goes to their heads and they are off on rampages, wilding madly, reeling and screeing like drunken sailors on shore leave, driving every cardinal and winter robin from the harvest of sweet fruit, which, they claim louder than ever, is theirs and theirs alone. Now chaos and old night reigns: bodies careen against glass, some break their necks trying to roister their own splendid images, and for a moment the world is put under grievous erasure. Orgy of greed and excess, we say. The insistent *me, me, me* turned now to this: renegade feathers drift down, settling like a dust of snow on our window ledges, sticking like lacy gray blossoms in the bare limbs of ironwood, fire bush, hawthorn, and forsythia. Later, because we are not sure we will love each other any more or less tomorrow, we step outside to count corpses, each with its own tiny crimson jewel, a single bead of blood clasped at beak's tip. Look, we say, this could be our body, this the sign of our flesh, *if only, if only, if only....*

NORTH

"How beautiful the scene is, and a little terrible...."
—Robinson Jeffers

How scenes shift, turn tail on themselves, like today, driving gravel ridge roads in the hilly part of our state, no other way possible to get where I was going. Four or five lefts here and five or six rights there, more zig-zag than arrow shot, and suddenly half a century lies in my lap, pelted back through *swish, swish* of windshield wipers. So much rain one long ago month that sea and sky bled into each other, one moment resembling the next, interchangeable, ubiquitous, and even our bickering in close quarters of father's old coupe turned familiar, its own reason for being, the radio's static fueling acrimony among dead-end passages, round-about highways, haphazard detours. Provincial roads obliterated, hills, cliffs, trees awash, and air itself a sodden grey, like an unending horizon of dusk, dingy under blanketed clouds, and under that sunless sky, every river in spate, brown, roily, except for this: relentless push and urge of salmon as long as our legs hydroplaning in the streets of coastal villages, salmon as thick as our waists turning up like holiday surprises in citizens' rec rooms, pantries, bathtubs, garages, and everywhere in the water-borne towns, children in outsized oilskins awake at first light, whacking great silvery fish on their heads with baseball bats or spearing the wriggling bodies with gaffs and spiked poles, as bloodstains spread like blooming flowers and lace filigree in estuaries and rivulets, creeks and storm drains. Then children loaded fish after fish in toy wagons, or stuffed their bodies in grain sacks, carried away to be emptied, corpses stacked and sorted like cord wood, eventually smoked and dried, every ounce destined to feed something, the pink delectable flesh to their families, who will not have eaten in this way for a generation, the bones and gill plates and offal slopped into reeking compost piles, to be turned by hand, laboriously, and spread on acres of potato fields, corn swales, soy bean carpets to enrich the harvest in late summer, to make up what little can be made up when water without end comes to turn its tricks, when water without end reaps what it sows.

A River In Wyoming

—for Louis Owens (1948-2002)

Delicious reverie: those stolen hours studying topo maps, tracing a thin blue or red line squiggling toward blank spots, remote, uninhabited places, where, happy to say, the road—"unimproved" our Forest Service declares—is an afterthought: washed out, rocky, root strewn, as gnarled and crooked as a heart in hiding, rough beast ready to spring. North Cascades, Sierras, San Juans, Absarokas, Big Horns: that's where we want to be, going always already toward headwaters, strong medicine in every language, laying lost or almost forgotten, between rigid coordinates of latitude and longitude. You knew the drill better than most: follow that line as far as your wheels will take you, then shoulder the packables, further, to trail's end, set up camp, and head for the river to read there in the mesh of your seine net grammars of possibility: stonefly larva, caddis pupa, and those mayfly nymphs, whose rude humped bodies, soon to sprout wings, will ride the current like so many tiny sun gods in silken boats, imperial ephemera, here now, then gone in the blink of an eye. Brief and glorious transit: the way of things, we say, the world reduced to sheer appetite. Louis, is it all we can expect these latter days, like that shuddering moment at dusk along a willow-choked bank when a coyote appeared with a snake in its mouth? Startled, I minded then how the world goes on immediately afterward, I minded well then how nothing matters, or everything does. Who decides? It was nearly dark. One more try, I promised, and cast the dark fly onto darker water. A trout struck, the water frothed: it was a cutthroat, 14 maybe 15 inches long, native to these regions, bright orange slash beneath its jaw—a prize in this small river. It was dark, I was hungry. Something moved in the vast night sky: it might have been an airplane, or satellite, or God's eye winking in interstellar dust. I was hungrier than I had ever been: I thought *why not?* and let the fish go. It hung in current then disappeared.

At The Armor Museum

> "Dust is the only secret."
> —Emily Dickinson

Bite and snarl of jackhammers up and down narrow city streets when you rose from sweet sleep in a huff, neighborhood all around you backhoed piece by piece onto dump trucks and hauled to landfills or road construction sites in Ayer or Leominster. *Progress*, the city fathers claimed, *out of sight, out of mind,* they said, except for the wake of concrete dust settling gray and gritty in your rented rooms, on the few cheesy things you call your own, on every leaf on every tree in a three block radius. Even birds' throats stopped in the endless grind of machines, though once in awhile you thought you heard a familiar call from your rural past—a catbird's rusty creak, like an unoiled hinge or visor opening and closing in pre-dawn moil beneath the oddball courtyard magnolias. You were twenty, worked as a door-to-door salesman for a fly-by-night company there's no need to name at this late date. Let's say, among other things, without being overly petty, you hated the mandatory dress code, the suit jacket's thin lapels, garish striped tie. That and the crap you had to peddle, the shit you had to eat. Every morning the same thing: every morning in the hallway mirror you met yourself coming and going, every morning in the scalloped glass you saw a body cobbled together with odd parts of different people—scarred feet flat as boards, ankles like softballs, fly-away ears, balloon nose, pocked skin, thin, unruly hair, and inside your skull, a maniac's brain—like a Gothic medical experiment gone crazy. Every morning was one of those days you dreaded and only promised to get worse. You had no inkling what today's or next year's story would be, but, life being too much with you, over lunch hour's thin fare in the shadows of the armor museum, you plotted deep-sixing your boss with a broad sword, changing your name to Lance, growing a nut-brown beard, and riding south, where, tanned and imperially slim, breast plate and helmet polished to a gleam, you would fall upon the thorns of life, etc., etc., in proper tragic form defending a suitably gorgeous, adoring woman's honor, etc., etc. Mostly, though, you seethed, you fumed, you boiled, and through it all dismantling went on and on that year in Worcester, Massachusetts, dust falling through high peaked skylights, dust settling like ash on marbled hallways, dust blanketing acres of chain mail and steel-clad torsos, dust crooning its long drift of regret, and nothing in your life about to change.

The Year Dylan Went Electric

—for Tom, Ron, Steve

An exaggerated scene, faded concert footage, you return to looking for clues: something like how who you were became who you might have been, something like memory and its discontents: the blue and the black, the hell to pay. Someday you'll figure out you are your own answer but then, after a night of special excess at Boynton Tavern, after way too many beers and shots to dull the pain of a woman you thought you loved moving out, after way too many pickled eggs, and a belly full of loose fuck-talk with a gang of wet-dream buddies, you stumbled out alone, no one else in tow, dust swirling upward with each step down wind-blown streets. Home, such as it was, then: suddenly, for no logical reason except that you thought you should make up for lost time (lost how? lost to whom?), you grabbed your landlord's battered upright from its place on the stairs, and began vacuuming your rooms, vacuuming in pitch dark. Just like that, spur of moment, without fanfare or premeditation, and no one to see, really, only a drunk-dumb audience of one. It seemed like the only thing to do: loud enough, too, to wake the dead, but you didn't care, impulsive bastard, because for a few minutes, in its whine and roar you were out there ahead of everyone else, at stage edge, without backup, going for broke: master of your fate, viceroy to a tiny universe of need. Admit it: in those clamorous moments you loved the reaper's single eye, more dazzling than the gaze of the all-knowing upon a desert wilderness. That, yes, plus the sexy, righteous way it took what it wanted, no questions asked, no apologies tendered: how it sucked up with impunity each foreign object, each piece of highlighted lint, speck of petrified food, tarnished earring, iridescent ant. Breadth and scope of the all-mighty: in the land of soot and dust Hoover ruled, queller of disorder, imperial collector of secrets, destroyer of alien detritus. Back and forth, up and down, through bedroom and hallway, each sculpted line on the frayed brown carpet a victory against that junk in your heart, snake coiled in your throat. Ride that beast, bucko: no more Mister Nice Guy for you, not then anyway in full fret and frenzied throb of your bully machine, never again *let sleeping dogs lie.* Not you. Not ever.

THE INVENTION OF CRUELTY

We heard about him first before we saw him, The Noted Writer. Heard that he was in town and headed our way by private limo (though years later people who said they knew better swore he arrived by helicopter). As I say, in the rumor mill, his fame definitely preceded him. We couldn't help but hear that he was headed our way whether we were ready for him or not (and most, myself included, I am not ashamed to say, were not fully, completely). When Himself (he was much smaller than I imagined) was ushered into the hushed room, I forget by whom, just a little more than an hour late, his yellow hair looked sullen (someone said it had a mind of its own), but there was no mistaking that his wrinkled skin, that famous craggy skin, smiled at us (we learned later it too had a mind of its own), and those pale eyes, we all agreed emphatically, Oh, those blue, blue eyes—droopy lids, long exquisite lashes and all—took us in without comment and went straight through Mandy, Priscilla, and Tim (they confessed later). I think he was in it for our hearts. Yes, I am as sure of that as I am of anything: he was out for our hearts. He trafficked in hearts, our teacher said, so watch yours, keep it close. Yes. I'd done my homework, after a fashion, dipping here and there into a recent opus of his magnificent canon. Speaking only for myself—and now, I admit, it gets ticklish—I *wanted* to lose my heart. I couldn't imagine not losing it (at least if not then, then later, but that is another story.) At first our Magisterial One was silent, an old owl blinking in infernal sun. Someone, Randy, or maybe Keisha, I think it was, whispered he looked nervous, though I am not so sure. A man like that, how could it be? After a few glasses of Sherry—or maybe it was Port—his tongue loosened and he warmed to his words which is after all why we were there then, all of us rank amateurs in the trade and hungry for secrets that would make a difference. He told his story again (it had been in the glossy magazines—we all read it—and later he put it in his memoir with some small changes) of waking in a daze, his famous jowls—those celebrated jowls (you saw photos of them everywhere at Poetry Boutiques)—not knowing where he and they were. *You see how it is: they came with pike staffs and knee knockers because they thought why not they could do whatever they wanted and no one would stand up to them, not you, not me, no one....* His Eminence went on like that, speaking in riddles for another ten minutes. At first I didn't get the point. What's the point, I asked. It's the Ur-Story, our teacher said. The first day of the rest of your life. You mean our life, Chrissie piped up, but back then it was easier—far easier—to imagine such things happening in the body politic. Never mind. It was quite a performance. And though I am out of the trade (have been for a long, long time), my route having taken a turn I could never have then foreseen, I still think of him now and then alone in a starched bed in a glitzy big-city hotel in who-knows-what metropolis, noise of sirens piercing the sealed glass windows, the neon flash of TV bruising the flesh of his eyes. Yes, the poem of violence, I remember he called it, the poem of our time. *Let it come forth,* he said, *you will not stop it, no matter how hard you try.*

Rimbaud, Falling

—for Jim Harrison (1937-2016)

So: today you are thinking scars and maybe shadows, though there is little sun, and then huge flapping birds, say, vultures, coal-smudged, tar-feathered, on their way to who-knows-where? gliding (no, lurching) over spindly multiflora rose and blackberry cane, all the green (sparse here seems right) that's left in tracts of twice-cut woodlots, reaped without mercy (a damn shame you admit) in any country, whatever its name. And you: driving home, late afternoon, over ridge roads winding through Morgan County ("colorful Morgan County," brochures say), you, again, watch another late winter storm rise steeply over steep hills of southeast Ohio (named here not for the first or last time), as though, as though, the hand of someone you've just held , or you might once have known (maybe her, maybe not her)—yes, let's say, might once have known (you admit, then, to wanting that life?)—laid its cold hello everywhere at once, so all you pass, or passes you, sports a glaze, a glassy eye, a wanderer's ice-born gaze.

***

And so: even what's known you think is maybe unsayable after all: all along dirt haul roads, a few rough-hewn batten shacks still occupied, coal smoke rises slowly (can I say this?

may I say this? you wonder) in mulatto March light: just so high and no higher, then strung out in air, inverted now as you watch: a burley horizon makes and unmakes itself (for some reason you think of barrel chests, fat rumps), then at the margins you hear a lisp, a tongue slip, and not a place in the mind or heart unfazed by its stutter: which sounds like this (if memory serves): a long gasp, a mesmerizing tick deep in salt-flinched veins, a dead reckoning, or so you guess, pleased with yourself, more or less, now that you are on a roll and thinking of such things....

***

So now: "such things" as what's known is unsayable, though even philosophers take words (and more) to say that, to say that "what's known is unsayable." So why not begin again? Say you are only in the kingdom of ice and snow, the country of blank, and every day from now on (you promise not to forget this) you will use a different color, each day a new color, in passing order, like this: Tuesday blue, Thursday brown, or like this: Friday black, Sunday yellow, and so on, and so on, emerging this fracture of evening let's say, moody, hungry, from crude vigils the other side of like, other side of maybe.

Quadtych, With Place Names

1. Rise of the All-Girl Groups

And then, just when you least expect it, when you are all thumbs at some menial task in Norwalk or Secaucus, or, more likely, wherever you are, you have just been chastised by your wife or lover for being the this or that, the fill-in-the-blank, you really are, old memories rise, and the steady two-count beat, the simple harmony, spins up in your beleaguered head. Suddenly, for whatever it is worth, it's that era again, and you are back a lifetime ago in a cramped attic bedroom or dank cellar of a small, sharp-angled bungalow, dancing alone to radio music, dancing and singing like a maniac, alone with your slick sweat and off-key fantasy, your winged life. But you don't care because why should you? because in that one book of your life, the one you happened to be writing at that moment, and which you kept handy for just such occasions, they are always there, moving toward you in unison: hair teased, starched and piled high, hips like syrup, and names to be savored, as sweet as dessert—Chiffons, Ronnettes, Bobbettes, Supremes—sepia queens whose synchronized moves and low-down peach tree shaking brought an ache to your heart night after night, no one else to see or hear your antics, no one else to put an ear close to the shaded light and whisper *why?* or *don't*.

2. West 45th Street

I took my girl friend to the city. We drove down to Manhattan, had dinner, like two out-of-town big wigs, at The Cattleman on West 45th Street. As famous as it was, it's gone now, like Toots Shore's on 52nd, closed years ago, but I remember its dark oak-trimmed interior, its dim lighting, and bustle and hover of people paid to imagine they could make your life better or more pleasant, even for an hour or so. It was late Spring, I wore a lightweight putty-colored suit, a button-down Oxford shirt, and a rep tie—a standard Joe College uniform; she wore a spaghetti-strap floral dress, a silky blue shoulder wrap, and high heels. She was beautiful in a brilliant and unexpected way, like the long drifts of day lilies we saw lining the highway were brilliant and unexpected. You came around a corner and there they were, lighting up a whole hillside with their nodding faces. She could do that too, light up a whole place like it had never been lit up before. On the ride home, tie loosened, churning up the Merritt Parkway in my tiny car, I told her I loved her. Well, that's not quite right—what I told her was, "I'm crazy about you," which if I had thought about it or known better, was a different thing altogether. In her driveway we kissed. One of us—maybe both—still buzzed from wine, narcotic drive home, evening of excess fallen squarely in our laps, promised the moon before calling it a night. Her father was upstairs dying, I remember that, I remember us having to be quiet when I walked her to the door. I remember now her name was Mary Lou. We never saw each other again.

3. Ego et in Arcadia

Sure, there were stars in Los Gatos, I remember, and a scrim of lacy, fly-away clouds, and a deep, dark evening sky that went on forever above the jacaranda and bougainvillea. Their colors, their fragrances: yes, I remember all that, plus the waxing moon, bone white in its lusty cradle. And there was you and there was me, swimming in and out of shadows. I remember that too, the delicious feel of it all, as though it were something edible, or a dream with a velvet lining I waited a long, long time to enter. I was going to say that was the point, to savor it all, after too much denial and abstinence, too much banking of appetite, but now I'm not so sure. Pool, hot tub, teak deck, the whole sun coast deal. I could be making all of this up and except for you, now beyond speaking, who would know any better, who would be any wiser? I think I made you up in all your finery of flesh and hair. *Sumptuous* comes to mind, so does *bounteous*. Somewhere, though, in a ledger in someone else's hand, let it be written that you were right: doubt is my middle name, though others were involved in this project, whose names and faces receded long ago, wisps in a heat-knockered eye, arrows loosed at noon. Just you and me and friends and friends of friends, I think you called them, none of us, God forbid, on the road to Damascus. And yet this too: somewhere east of us, constant hum of freeway traffic, echoing off a backdrop of low-lying foothills, and beyond that, among stands of live oaks and gambols of scattered quail, horses passing toward the ocean in the ache of midnight. Let it be said I remember that too.

4. A Naturalist's Guide to the Topics

So that: all our lives a misreading: and here, within eyeshot of Stresa, sculpted among jeweled bays and stone-cropped islands, where they once set bow to winter breakers and trolled these waters for silver-scaled fish, she peers out of an enormous copse of summer hydrangeas, a mother-lode of pastels in every hue and shade: her place on earth, her patch of sacred soil, but happy or sad our book will not say, and her face and breasts will not say, either, bronze body pocked by age and turned inland away from sea walls and spiraling palms toward weathered doors, dull tin signs selling *dolce*. Even the myth about her, the long story of her opened hands, while not exactly dubious, is a clouded text, an uncertain gesture, stained by all the common usuals—greed, vanity, you name it (though even if you spoke their language, few citizens here would admit that), for, after all, they say, she is what she is and gives what she has, no more, no less. We came here expecting something else, found this instead: a winged life, a tear-lapped cheek, so make of it what you will, no more, no less.

Up Late Reading *Birds Of America*

> "...in my sleep I continually dreamed of birds."
> —John James Audubon

No need for alarm or clock radio today: at dawn, incessant *caw, cawing* of crows, savviest birds in Christendom, pulls you up from tidal suck of sleep into aviary of warped flights and body betrayals. In mind's eye, out there, roadside, beneath hoary chinquapin oak, a flattened mammal carcass, coon's or possum's (you don't know for sure), bully beak probing its brain, luckless upstaring marble eye a delectable plum or juicy oyster for morning's imperial scavengers, rising breeze now ruffling their gloss-black feathers, shimmering like darkened mylar in each turn of wind. The great spine-broke book still open on your chest, passion of color held tight in taloned grip, scapular shafts arrowing a printed page. Still groggy, see yourself, younger, almost unrecognizable, sleepwalking (if you want to think of it that way), coming toward home again, toward that small, sharp-angled suburban house at wood's edge, coming home again through nodding fox tail, head-high grass, plumed cattail stalks, foggy-headed, too, like this, having followed all day a commotion of crows until you found them dive bombing a lone barred owl (the first you had ever seen). Under a milky sky, whose pale ambient eye saw all and said nothing, you watched, wanderer, hidden in a tangle of crooked sumac and spiked hawthorn bushes, as the lumpen-bodied bird flew, crazed by crows, through dappled sunlight, a crook-winged fish in air, its palsied body tricked from dreamland, careening bedazzled from one tree to another, like a drunk stunned to silence when there is too little mercy to go around. What's done is done, though, and even now, in a whisk of breath, molted self slipping in and out of shadows, you belong to no one, yet go on reading, turning pages, humbled by each avian spectacle, still starved by the thing shrinking in your heart, the ruinous blank in your eye, the empty *whathaveyou*, let's say, like birds' riotous language, meant now, you see, only to tease and bedevil, nothing more, nothing less.

During A War

—for Mark, John, Lars

We were gathered around our hosts' dining room table, a group of us revelers. This was after champagne in their living room, in front of a fieldstone fireplace that reached to the rafters. Did I say it was a new house, a new airy house in the country, with killer views? A few fieldstones, rough to the touch, still sported tiny colonies of moss. Everyone remarked, especially the city dwellers among us: look how positively wonderful, they said, and several, thinking it would make a difference, carried water to the stones' lips, so the homely tufts would never ever lose their spunk. But water missed its mark, ran crazily down to the floor, gathered in small puddles by our feet. Enough is enough, some quipster said, let was be the finale of is.

***

As I was saying, we were gathered around our hosts' dining room table, a group of us revelers. There were several who were not there around the table with us and of course they were dearly missed. Remember this one, remember that one, we said. We thought about them, then raised our glasses heartily, cheerfully, around the long harvest table, spoke their names more or less in concert. Did I say it was Thanksgiving? It was also someone's birthday, which happened to fall exactly on Thanksgiving Day every seven years, I think it is. This was a seventh year double whammy—national holiday and birthday on the very same day: it doesn't get much better than that, someone said between fork fulls. Wait, yes it does: this was actually a triple whammy, because it wasn't just any routine birthday, but a landmark birthday, too, you know, like 21, 40, or in this case 60. The Big Six-0, our host said, reaching for the gravy boat. The table was piled high in that American way, not so much with bounty as with spoils: now the cave of the turkey's breast cavity yawned darkly, the great knuckle of ham gleamed like a decapitated head. And in their burnished pans and barrows, the once-bounteous mounds of stuffing, mashed potatoes, peas and onions, cranberry sauce were reduced to smidgens. And though no one could eat another morsel, over on the sideboard, for all to behold, the desserts lolled on their cooling rack, five kinds of pie calling to stopped ears, a chilled fruit-laden Jello mold shimmering in elegant candle light, and an outsized chocolate cake ribbed with white icing, its crown bedecked with birthday script.

***

At our hosts' dining room table, someone broke out the dope, a chunk of opiated hash, of all things, delivered, believe it or not, by courier no less from the Kingdom of Morocco. I know whose it was, but won't tell, because, well, it has nothing to do with this. We *oohed* and *aahed*, we passed the tiny pipe, we smoked, we coughed, our eyes glazed, we fell silent, moved inward, each and every one of us on our own flight of fancy. The tall tapered candles drew down to their ends, and blue wax dripped to the table cloth. Later, in unison we threw our flute-stemmed glasses into the firebox to christen the house, our hosts' new lives there at the edge of those burly woods. The fire hissed and sputtered. It was late November, someone bet it would snow soon, and others said no, not yet, not in this part of the state. Outside, in a milky wash of patio light, two flying squirrels came down a tree trunk then glided to the bird feeder. Their round black eyes took us in. No one moved. No one said a goddamn word.

The Dredge At Alder Gulch

So, they came into the valleys, following ridge lines, deer paths, corduroy roads: they came into valley towns and outlying hamlets at night, hauling their equipment, hiding in their own shadows. It didn't matter how they got there, they slipped past everyone, even the watchers assigned to watch, and they got where they were going anyway, by hook or by crook. They came always from somewhere else, because they thought why not? Why do unto your private patch what you can do to a stranger's? So they came from somewhere else carrying their own shadows, hauling their equipment, because they were on the hunt and thought, who is awake enough to stop us? Like spoiled children, they acted as though there would be no end to their fun. They did not bother with right and wrong, and certainly the equipment they brought did not know right from wrong, but like them, the massive machines they brought were great with appetite, but not conscience, and devoured everything in sight: first it was gold they lusted after, then silver, and when that, too, hid from their eyes, they lowered their eyes and went after rubies and garnets. Then, it was stands of trees, both deciduous and evergreen, and every gradient thereof measured in raw board feet, and when there wasn't enough to go around and the hillsides and swales were laid bare and no avian chorus sang in the graveyard of stumps, and at last everyone thought their hunger was sated, well, then their maws opened wider and they developed a taste for earth itself: deep running coal veins, gravel banks, and every sorry thing that stood in their way: streamside vegetation of every hue and fiber, and even the tiny insects, smaller than motes of dust, less weighty than a filament of hair, went through the belly wringer, and after that the bright-colored fish that had lived in riffles and runs since the last ice age soon were no more, because every crooked creek and stream and meandering river and dog-legged watercourse had been gutted by the furious, smoking engines of want. It happens everywhere—interlopers get a taste for the things of the earth and what the things of the earth can bring them and they think why stop now? Let's keep going, let's take the machines where machines have never been before. Whatever the great beasts touched turned to trash, whatever they belched became poison, whatever they did lived on afterwards etched in acid and rust, wherever they moved, the same scoriations of earth in the name of greed and prosperity, the usual fucking suspects.

Near Last Chance

South of here, in counties angled like tin sheets in the merciless sun, someone refused to listen and went on shaving the land wafer-thin year in and year out anyway for the sake of family and increased yield. Savvy neighbors—men and women just like our parents, no better no worse, hoeing that same row for who knows what or why?—saw a righteous thing had been done and they followed suit, ridding their land of fencerows, plowing wall to wall. *God knows,* someone wrote, *we do what we can to live.* It went on like that for a long time until the wind came and blew all day and all night and into the next day and night too. It was the talk of the land, and in churches preachers harangued the people for not loving their earth enough to make it stay home and behave: *Please, Jesus, help us restore dominion over this bastard earth,* they said in towns where potato and hops were king. But dirt had a will of its own, fell in love with wind, packed its bags, turned to dust, and lit out. And soon layers of ash, where the land had scorched, and heart soil, where roots had once spread, these too blew away, and migrated hundreds of miles north and east, hiding the mountains and blanketing lakes with their smoky gaze. And willows and yews flattened in the unstoppable gusts and blue pines shook so hard their tops snapped, and the eyes of fish hawks and night-grazing deer began to burn like cataracts in the undammed river of dust. Then the sky itself became a hoax, small birds could not fly above and so lay down in sere grass and weeds and trembled in their gritty clothes, which gave new meaning to dusting, that no amount of preening could cure. And when dust was everywhere dust could go or be, the people pleaded ignorance first then outrage, for it had never been this way. Dust everywhere, dust passing through glass and metal, dust refusing to quit or know its place, dust swirling and billowing with impunity, dust sneaking like thieves, like murderers, into our hearts, into the secret places where we thought we thought we still lived.

At The Turn Of This Century

1. Breviary

Just like that, a northern clipper, a monster blizzard from Alberta, a place I've never seen and know less about, rolled across the heartland into my back yard, like it had something against me and mine and was out to even a score. *Bam!* Snowfall like a fist in the face when I woke to find a present I hadn't ordered delivered, believe it or not, on time for once: *winter here, winter there, winter, winter everywhere.* I should have been shoveling snow or hanging strings of cheery lights. I could have been writing gay holiday greetings, decking halls with fragrant boughs, or brewing a hot toddy against so much polar bluster. Instead, I braved the elements, crouched low behind pillar and post to watch the feathered tribe flock to my feeders. I made a list and checked it twice because why not, it was a day to remember, bird-wise anyway: yellow-bellied sapsucker northern flicker american goldfinch northern cardinal eastern towhee eastern bluebird black-capped chickadee slate-colored junco white-breasted nuthatch downy and hairy and red-bellied woodpeckers blue jay white-crowned sparrow mourning dove house finch carolina wren then a lone sharp-shinned hawk scaring the bejesus out of the banqueters, except the tufted titmice, grey-and-white cavaliers, quick puffs of smoke, carrying us all, neighbors now, toward dark with their insistent *peter, peter, peter, peter…*

2. Representatives are Standing By

Gnarled oak casts its shadow on the bedroom wall: last light of day passes into deep ether of space and we are left to our own devices and what little we can fall back on under winter's humped dome, its snow globe effect: in the shake of flurries, nothing elegant, you understand, no filigrees or embroidery on the smooth stitch of our eyes, and certainly no enchantments this far in the game, just snow as it is, snow in snowy fields, snow in snowy trees, snow stacked on snowy rooftops and phone wires, as usual this late in the day its color shading toward blue, then blue-black like a bruise, not a trick of optics, as some might have told you, but banishment of white when evening lays down its blanket and Earth spins toward midnight, the hard-buckled belt all along the line of descent cinching tighter, the gap between *out there* and *in here* growing smaller, while darkness enters our veins, fills empty corridors of our heads, as doors in long passageways bang open, making way for a body—whose we cannot say—sleepwalking, palsied by pain, say, or turned to forgetfulness in deepest hours of star-cold night.

3. Solstice

Up way past midnight with Dickinson again, mouthing poem 258, chewing on it, worrying its cold bone, rehearsing for no reason the sixty-one second minute only an imperial watchmaker, regulator of our atomic clock, will care about or even notice at year's end. When the time comes, like most citizens of our Republic, I'll squander my extra second, throw it away with impunity, and perhaps even a flair of insouciant profligacy. I admit, I've been rotten that way my whole life, wasting all manner of things I'll never get back. No surprise then after fitful night's sleep, I rose late, still groggy, with sun already hovering in weak, watery sky. Deferral, or is it denial, the rule of this briefest day? No breakfast yet, but coffee in hand, mind sloshing this way and that, down to shuttered work room: small aperture on smaller world, slanted inward ("Where the Meanings, are," she says) toward a banked fire, heat fading from wavering ashes, and my thick-coated dog nuzzling my crotch with her leathery nose, still cold from sleeping under stars. She circles the carpet as dogs have always done, drops down in a patch of fugitive sunlight, licks her vulva, preens for ten minutes, then sleeps again, curled nose to tail, composed like a minor deity, a painted figure, like time, beyond comprehension, beyond all need to explain herself, though even if she could, at this late hour, would anyone be listening ?

Nebraska Letter

—for Beef Torrey (1958- 2013)

I write from the sadness of the heartlands, country of covered malls, ethanol, and sluggish rivers, where what happened happened that day I was planning to cash out. You couldn't stop me, even if you'd known. I admit, in the global scheme of things, nothing spectacular or world shaking took place, you understand, just a last minute swerve after the razor was stropped and honed to a diamond edge, and my affairs, less messy, I think, than usual, were tied with a silky ribbon. I'd left instructions for all who cared to read them: notes on scraps of colored paper tacked brightly like autumn leaves, I thought, all over house and grounds, perfectly placed, I thought, to catch a reader's eye: this valve leaks something awful, one read; another, feed birds only at night, and a third (of many, many): blue is my favorite color. Friend, all that scribbling and busyness sidetracked me, which explains nothing except my own fickleness, though I know you might put another spin on it.... Don't stop me even if you will have heard this before. For diversion, as I went scribbling between pillar and post, I often stooped low to listen for mice and voles thieving in burrows beneath my iris corms and lily roots. It was just a game at first, but what the hell, it's all in the ears, I remember thinking: look what owls and foxes can do with a blanket of snow on the ground, how they hone in on the tiniest nerve vibration or infinitesimal heart beat, rising toward them like a shout from a world acres beneath this one, where when something moves, stirs ever so slightly in pitch darkness, in absolute (to us) darkness of nothing, they cock their weapons, shoot, and ask questions later. I know that, I've seen those nature shows: great gray owl dive bombing a miserable rodent through a yard of snow, the arctic fox arcing like an Olympic diver before plunging into snow two feet deep. All anyone can say, I guess, is that one thing leads to another: I like best that those victims never know what's coming, then *blam*, the roof caves in and a tooth razors clean through brain pan, a talon opens a river of blood, its pooling stain almost lost in all that blankness. On tv the killers nearly always come up with dinner, but that day, hard as I tried, I rose empty from table. By then it was dusk, a hint of snow was in the air, but I didn't care: I lay on my belly, cold grass in my face, ear pressed to the rotten earth. When I mouthed my portion of dirt and detritus, the only sound was wind rattling seed stalks and raspy heads of teasel at wood's edge. I think I was lucky. You can't fake that.

The World Is But Whirligig

Someone I know (not exactly a friend but then not a stranger either), a friend of a friend, I'll call him, though I admit I don't hear from very often, writes from the hinterlands: *one thing leads to another,* he says. and out of the blue, just like that, he's bought for next to nothing an empty grain elevator (of all things) with a perilously tall ceiling. This is in a tiny rural town I have no reason ever to visit, and though I am not sure why he tells me this (I hear he's a guarded man) says he plans to use it as a studio where he can *stretch* (his word) and do arty things like paint or write or carve wooden birds when the spirit moves him (I hear from a friend of another friend this splashy new life is really to escape his wife, who has always worn the pants in his family, not, I suppose, that there is anything wrong with that). But before I get too far behind myself, here's the point: snow on my pal's part of the Great Plains is so deep he can't get out of his yard and drive to the next town to kick start his bright idea. Isn't that always the way? What comes at us comes at us from such weird angles and then leaves us, flies out the window before we're certain what we've seen or heard. *The way we miss life is life,* my friend's friend says. Maybe that's how I know it's probably 30 or more below (my mind runs to extremes) lots of places on our great spinning earth ball, but I don't care, because today right here in the Hocking River valley the sun keeps climbing, the temperature keeps rising. *Unseasonable,* the local paper calls our thaw. Two weeks ago winter was wintering like a champ the way it should this time of year: gutters and downspouts froze solid, daggers of ice hung from every inch of our soffits, and shallow-rooted trees toppled in backyard woodlots, ice and snow pulling them down like the weight of regret or ignorance (no one was sure which). I sat tight for what seemed like a long time, brewed green tea, cooked lentil soup, ate no red meat or God forbid, *foie gras*, vowed never to talk trash again, fed the fire stick by thorny stick, hunkered down under woolen blankets, and waited for the jet stream to change its mind. Finally, it blew our way and in no time we were basking, as I say, in all manner of warmth and sunshine. I let the fire go out and got busy right away doing spring chores in mid-January, things you just don't see people doing until April or May in these parts. I stripped down and went forth to pick up windblown debris and downed limbs from my yard, tamp down frost heaves, straighten garden fences, mulch perennial beds with cedar chips and fresh straw, scrub the dog kennel with bleach, fill bird feeders to overflowing. I had a busy day of it improving my lot, detail by detail, inch by inch, as I think we all should. Before one thing leads to another, don't ask reasons why, I say, take what you're given and don't look a gift thaw in the mouth.

Moscow: Novodevichy Convent

Grey the sky, grey the stone ramparts above Chekhov's and Gogol's graves, and the lumpen resting places of wayward virgins, disobedient daughters of high and mighty families buried here for four centuries, accidents of history in today's planetary autumn freeze sweeping toward Moscow from distant steppes: juggernaut of cloud and wind and snow blown from Kamchatka Peninsula and Vladivostok, across boreal forests and wheat fields, over the tattered body of Mother Russia. From here in morning's broken light it might be a Kandinsky painting: jumbled panorama of rust-angled crosses—souvenirs of collective resistance and pitched battles—lean toward earth, and beyond, paper-yellow aspens disrobe along the Moscow River, dark welt, long, looping bruise, in the middle distance, now Hollywood's outpost, a movie set for badly written novels. Nothing is as we expected: missiles point inward, market stalls are empty, citizens wander cobbled streets looking for scraps of bread, anything to eat or to barter. The rag merchant and hoodlum dictate fashion. Nothing is as it seems, our new friends warn us, and before every ruble turns to dust they want what they want, desire without end like us, they say over and over. We know this, know it is prudent to hang onto our hearts anyway. Remember how we tried? When I left you at dawn, the sweat of your breasts was still sweet in my mouth, the honey of your vagina still hot and fragrant on my lips and fingers. When I left you so early this morning, a thinly dressed stranger on the strangest of streets, I heard lamentations rising like birds' cries, and fell in with a funeral procession, wheeled cart and all, winding its way to this house of sorrow. Oh, the coldness of this place! I wish you had warned me: how it rises through the floor up my feet and legs, into my scrotum, up my spine and into the empty rooms of my head. I wish you had told me how stone and mortar intensify chill, hold it, savor it as we once savored iced caviar. What do you think: could my stopping here have been fate? I should be dressed in rough woolens, yeoman's cap, heavy boots. Then I, too, might pass for another grieving comrade at death's stone altar. Larceny, I am sure, has nothing to do with it. Outside, below steep convent walls, five pairs of swans, arresting in their black plumage, bob, dip, and circle to keep a hole open in morning's icy stare. They mate for life, what they know is written in their genes. They act as if they forget nothing.

Christmas This Year

"The sudden silent trout are all lit up hanging, trembling...."
—Virginia Woolf, *To the Lighthouse*

Christmas morning, year of our lord two thousand and something and something. Woke alone this holy morning in a silent house to see neighbor's porches strung with festive lights, and another wrapping of snow on the tall grasses and stream-bent willows of nearby water meadows, now home to scurrying voles and night-hunting owls, all still tucked in their blue mangers, waiting. Place and time rise to a shape before anything else: geography of loss or season of plenty—what's the difference to reckless hearts? A cock pheasant crows from a far field, staccato interlude this early before the holiday world here comes back to itself. Then quickly there is wood smoke, more snow in the air, children's voices carrying down the tree-arched road. The elementals you would call them, landscape and consciousness, exponential increases of country living, less or more than the sum of, I was never quite sure. I confess my ignorance because I can't think of a reason not to. I'll admit it, I have nothing else but what I am about to tell you. There was no procession to midnight mass, no presents to exchange this morning over champagne and medallions of chocolate. Instead I went straight for the river, where it comes out of the millrace and flows south between stone walls and hedgerows, its vaporous breath rising slowly this cold dreamless day. Beneath a quaint stone bridge light bent across a deep pool, its edges laced with ice and spent bodies of tiny snow flies: watery chiaroscuro, black and white photo I might have taken had I had my wits about me. I waded in and cast a Brassie, a midge pattern not much heftier than an eyelash, or sliver, or grain of sand. The nymph drifted slowly, deeply through long winter shadows. It began to snow harder. How trout see a mote in God's eye, a speck of dust in their sunless firmament, is beyond me. I was lucky: trout wanted that fly today. Ice formed on my rod guides, my hands were numb, I missed strikes, but finally, when I stopped thinking, one came to hand. I laid the trout on the snowbank, unhooked the fly from its thin lip. In that trembling light he shone like a hand-painted ornament: tinseled body sprinkled with jet-black spots, sides crimson striped. I wish you had seen it, wish you had touched it before I sent it back home. Christ, I wish I wasn't writing this to kill time.

In Our 75th Winter

—for Dave and Dee Smith

Today, friends, because we have been out of touch for a long time (my fault, I admit, and the result not so much of sheer inertia but other things I don't care to go into, except to say body betrayals were involved), you ask me now to *hurry, hurry* with all the goings-on of our latter days, and so here I am at last with the very latest news. A few days ago, dawn-break sun slanted over my shoulder as I sat at my desk, pen in hand, thinking of you and yours, and though back yard trees were utterly bare, our maples, silver-gray in that pewter light, led me to believe we might have an early spring to celebrate.

***

Today, though, no sun is visible, and the jet stream, completely ass-backward for this time of year, blows toward us out of your region, carrying its airborne cargo of hammers and tongs. The mercury is *plummeting* according to our local weather maven, whose voice sounds indescribably sexy when she warns her flock of violent weather. *Whiteout*, she says breathily, and *wind chill*, savoring its jagged edges, then *blizzard*, my favorite, her voice razoring just so on the double *z*, then falling, in perfect ecstatic pitch. She has a swan's neck, straight red, red hair, and an angular face with what some might call *peaches and cream* complexion, though I like to think *ivory* comes closer to the mark. Yes, I'm sure *ivory* fits her much better. Once, I saw her at the paint counter of a local hardware store. I nearly threw caution to the wind and introduced myself (though she wouldn't have known me from Adam), but you know me, hesitant to fault—instead I peeked sidelong and fell into her eyes anyway: deep, deep pools, brilliant *oceanic green*. (Take my word for it, had you seen them you would know what I am talking about).

***

Today, she broadcasts an update every 30 minutes. If I were betting man I'd swear her nipples rise and harden in all that cold-chatter, all that storm lingo, though here I could be projecting my geezer's mind of winter on hers. I admit it: violent weather excites me, too—all that talk of extreme isobars, falling barometers, low pressure systems—what does it say of me that I prefer watching a killer storm, glorying in a hurricane's eye, or the monumental swath of a polar vortex, to a quiet evening *tête-à-tête*? Never mind: since dawn the temperature has dropped 40 degrees. Ice needles rattle every window. Lights flicker on and off. The road in front of our house has disappeared without trace, the city plows, stopped in their tracks down hill, cannot reach us.

***

Today, my snow queen, my ice princess, my archangel of weather, says it will only get worse, that we should try to stay *comfy* inside. (You would love the note of concern in her voice.) Let it come, then. Some dishes are best served cold: today's is the blue plate special: ice and its specific gravity, ice and snow and their power to hurt.

Falling Asleep Over Lowell

Yellowhammers patrician Lowell called them: their *yuck-a, yuck-a, yuck-a* echoed in mansions of hardwoods, raged like fire in air itself, some sort of *ars poetica* about his times, a sonic hieroglyph, say, or palimpsest of violent transport: yellow light of wings, lick of yellow flame, carried back and back, flickering at margins of another finger-worried text, another box inside the box. Amid funeral pyres, clanging armor, "Uncle Charles" this and "Mother's great-aunt" that, legions of bluebloods retired under the earth then and then, and the rest of us, blood-born too, but interlopers, latecomers, despised, reviled in our own way, boot gagging our throats, like some old man, baby-drooling over some hero book, some cockeyed modern *Aeneid*, a pretend princeling, dark guinea, on the lam from Sunday services or the weary whatever, still dreaming of *fatherland, motherland, home, family* in the old language.

* * *

So few trained classically any more, who cares, we say, that the sun no longer falls scarlet and blue on our page? Now, as a new century turns, in country where elm and oak forests have vanished, scrub apple clearings gone under tractor blades, yellow-shafted flickers are scarcely seen or heard. More's the pity, some say, a sign of our times: skewed climate no less than whacked-out policy to blame, but now and then as we drift through a vacant afternoon, intent on playing steward of the land, however small our parcel, or acting shepherd of the flock, however few, we think we hear that *yuck-a, yuck-a* chorus but aren't sure, a trick of wind or distance perhaps on a blowsy spring day....

***

One possible music of woodsy edges and greenbelts, we think, no more or less, just a lost accompaniment to reverie as we hunker down and regard that other book, too, by no means complete, a page-turner that rises from within, pitched in lengthening shadows as we listen now as others must have listened to feathers falling: hearing but not hearing, holding our breath, as though we might be someone else, some startled spank-ass do-gooder or cranky ne'r-do-well on the civic roles, hearing at last in our inner ear what our life has become in a new country.

It Is What It Is

"That's just love sneaking up on you..."
—Bonnie Raitt

Stars gathered beyond tattered cloud scrim and updrifting sparks from a bonfire in the backyard pit. Nighthawks cruised star roads above our heads, then gradually, a blink here, a blink there, fireflies winked in near darkness, as we fed the blaze stick by stick, hand over hand with attic junk and detritus left over from five moves in four years, the weight of stuff even a house that size could no longer bear: heaped newspapers, old love letters, cheap dresser drawers, plastic lawn chairs, and those glitzy magazines that burned a thousand shades of blue and red. Friends and strangers showed up too, damn near the whole hamlet, adding their two cents, for what it was worth. There we were, all of us making merry like champs and you the center of it all, dressed so ravishingly in low slung everything, burning like a streaking comet. We drank and drank and smoked and smoked ourselves silly, summer night fire roaring in fieldstone pit, beer, wine, and whiskey passed hand to hand and swigged in gulps, and then not long after all talk turned randy: who fucked whom, who ate whose pussy, who got a blowjob, at work no less. We learned so much about your neighbors. It went on like that for hours, nighthawks long since retired, lightning bugs switched off until next time. You made gaga eyes at me, one thing led to another, and before the last pyromaniac went home, we were currying smoke out of each other's hair. Naked, you dozed in mid sentence, head propped against my chest, your breasts floating above waterline, luscious islands of flesh: my hands cupped them, my fingers rolled your nipples gently. It went on like that for who knows how long, the candle slowly gasping to a nub and the tub water cooling, until, at last, shivering, you woke and turned toward me, more question than answer. Outside, in the dawn-wet woods, the one-eyed dog—your old brindle-colored hound—was running like a son of a bitch, chasing some primal thing, his voice orgasmic when he hit hot scent, just before plunging out of hearing.

Yellow Trillium Brown Trout Rusty Spinner

—for Earl DuBack (1942 -2019)

You know that time of year: hardly a murmur at first, no more than a stutter at best, that baseboard hum and mumble carries on for a few weeks, loud then soft, back and forth, all the live leafy things and their kin playing hide and seek, dawdling like slow pokes tying their laces, and even phoebes—they of the thinnest flute music—skimping and saving their pennies for a nest to be plastered for safety's sake under abandoned barn eave or out-of-the way bridge abutment. You know it goes on that way a long time near water courses, tall timber, and low hills—a stutter here, a shimmer there—stasis reigns, monotony is king. Then one morning you wake at dawn to green fuse bursting in every nook and cranny, every bird in Christendom trilling its feathered head off, and suddenly, without asking your permission, the world in the small place you live jolts and jives too fast to be held back, though you—already backward looking—are lamenting the moment's passing, the precise minute and second hence when it all comes to an end in an eye blink, and the world takes another turn without your consent. So it could have been wind-blown Montana or Utah, where light batters in from all sides without mercy, or the south counties of England—Walton country—in its lush spring finery, with monocled gents afoot on the close-mown berms, rods in hand, and not a hair out of place, but it wasn't.

Let's say this was near home on a quick-footed river in Appalachia, where you have no choice before now becomes then but to get with the speeding express, to put up or shut up, to fish or cut bait in this land of root and bud essentials that nervy theoreticians say don't exist. Earth, water, air: mayflies have been hatching all week in obscene numbers, true ephemerals, candles in the wind, lit and snuffed in mere hours, born without mouths and unable to taste, born only to fuck then to die. I was holding one, dead as a stone, in my heart. It might have been a question, something like whether we ever see ourselves in this picture, but I could be wrong. It was early May. I was supposed to be somewhere but forgot where, supposed to be with someone but forgot who. Maybe it was home, maybe it was not, maybe it was you, maybe it was not. I closed my eyes and tried to think of nothing beyond nothing. It was enough, I said, to stand in water where trout rose freely to sex-crazed Pale Evening Duns, trillium tipped their hats in profusion, and all around me streamside an audience of thousands watched the watcher.

Everything Gets Lost In Translation

> "I'll show you how to walk the dog..."
> —Rufus Thomas

I had a dog, a hunting dog, a blue Belton, though that doesn't give her her due, and nearly every day through the meat and bones of seasons I walked with her for hours from the bungalow, where someone I loved was dying, toward the pond at Allen's Meadows. We walked in good weather and bad, sun and rain, warmth and cold, dew and dust—twas all the same to her—through thick brambles and open fields, beneath choke cherry stands and sumac swales draped with bittersweet and snow, and out among the last swatches of native bluestem grasses in that small corner of the world. Dogs come and dogs go, we all know that, even great ones, the ones the dog men call brag dogs. I don't want to give her airs, but I think mine was a brag dog, too, as far as that went. She had brilliant confirmation—feathered tail like a high-hoisted flag, supple gait and fluid lines, dapple-colored muzzle, and syrupy brown eyes that drew you in whether you wanted to be drawn in or not. At heel she lazed and lolled, and matched me stride for stride, but when I released her with whistle blast or hand gesture, she became a burning comet, a hot-shot jet star, what dog men call a bold runner, capable of breaking hearts the moment she started her cast, sweeping into the wind, every nub and shank of nerve poised, alert, on guard. In a blink she was out alone in the stratosphere hunting like God's holy avenger, worrying every filament of air-borne scent, sniffing out every wild feathered thing in her path, and not giving a thought to her master. *The way of the world*, some say. *Same old same old*, some say. *Deal with it and move on*, some say. By now, maybe you have figured out these words are not about a dog and her owner and maybe never were. They're about how much time is left when days, then nights, line up against us, when everything passes through the eye of the needle, or nothing does.

In The Corner Room

> "An owl is an only bird of poetry"
> —Robert Duncan

Powdery snow on peaks above darkened river, hail, spilt like salt by an anxious guest, at feet of late-blooming roses, odor of bruised sage mingled with smoke from wood stoves down our gravel lane. On phone wires near the porch, tree swallows, arranged like notes on a page of sheet music, twitter and stir as evening comes on way too early and we turn up our lamps to see what yet can be seen. So now, bone-deep in another turning season, dusk, cloaked in deepening shades of rose and magenta, steals down hillsides and across waters, while a rising slivered moon, like a nail filing or crooked talon, catches itself in the jangled limbs of trees. Outside the corner room, its windows open to still-fragrant air, a clatch of great horned owls, burly home boys and their consorts, restless on their porches of pine and willow, strike up their bloody tune: *hunting will be good tonight*, it says over and over. Their litany echoes at the margins of sleep, that moment before the moment after, when the stirrings of everyone in the house settles to quiet as each sleeper prepares to enter the blue room inside their head, where who-knows-what gets into our dreams, where last night, in my dream, one yellow-eyed owl, fat as a Buddha, delivered mail on blue-black star roads across oceanic distances, and I read as though for the first time your last words: "Disappointed I've missed you the last few times you so kindly stopped by. In the north shadows, some snow. Rugged weather these past few weeks. Makes me wonder if our life on earth is truly blessed as the good books say, or whether it is only a brief dream, fearful and uncertain?" This time of year, asleep or not, words fall inward like scattered leaves, borne on cross-cutting winds into raw spaces marked by memory, for autumn is on its wings, and the road out of here, oiled and sinewy, cries out—toward us, toward you—to pack up and stow down before snow flies for good.

Robert DeMott was born in Connecticut in 1943, and schooled there, as well as in Massachusetts and Ohio. His poetry has appeared in *Georgia Review, Southern Review, Windsor Review, Ontario Review, Pittsburgh Quarterly, Quarterly West, Southern Poetry Review, Texas Review, North Dakota Quarterly, Cimarron Review, Tar River Poetry, Southern Humanities Review, Spoon River Poetry, Hiram Poetry Review, Lake Effect, Boolaboo, Crazy River, Sheila-Na-Gig online*, and elsewhere. He has published numerous books, including *Working Days: The Journals of* The Grapes of Wrath (a *New York Times* Notable Book), *Steinbeck's Typewriter: Essays on His Art* (recipient of the Nancy Dasher Book Award), *The Weather in Athens: Poems* (recipient of the Ohioana Award), *Angling Days: A Fly Fisher's Journals*, and *Conversations with Jim Harrison, Revised and Updated*. From 1969 to 2013 he taught at Ohio University, where he received half a dozen teaching awards. He serves on the editorial board of *Steinbeck Review*, and the directorial board of *Quarter After Eight*, a literary journal. He lives in Athens, Ohio, with Kate Fox, poet and editor.

About The Book

Each of these four-square, hybrid "proems," inspired in part by Audubon's great book, attempts to combine the amplitude and spaciousness of prose with the compression and focus of poetry. In traveling into the darkly intertwined spaces of personal geography, memory, emotion, and loss, as well as into wild nature, each piece surrounds its lyrical moment in a context of details, imaginings, and resonances to express its dramatic occasion.

"Bob DeMott's poems [in *The Weather in Athens*] achieve what is to me one of the most important accomplishments any poet can offer....We are invited to read through the screen of the words into the poem without being dragged back to the surface of the page by stylistic and graphic peculiarities. This is reader's poetry, inviting, heartfelt, generous and moving."

–Ted Kooser
Pulitzer Prize winner in Poetry
and former United States Poet Laureate

www.ingramcontent.com/pod-product-compliance
Lightning Source LLC
Chambersburg PA
CBHW060412080526
44583CB00012B/540